all at once

the poetry of

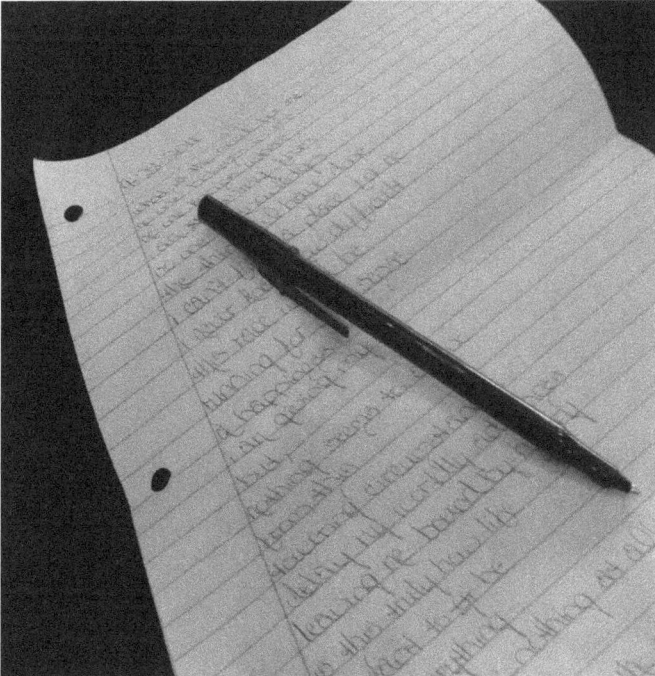

Kentrell Blanche

ISBN:
978-1-105-37608-5

Table of Contents

Roaming for Love

I was roaming the neighborhood
For love
When I came across your face;
I invited you into my life
And you quickly took your place..
You cancelled plans, made demands,
Juggled my life in your hands..
I wanted you to be *the one*,
I took pictures and I bragged;
I looked into your eyes
And thought I saw a star
But,
It was just a paper bag..
I fell, and I rolled
All over the ground;
I was flooded with emotion
But,
I dared not make a sound..
I found you while
Roaming the neighborhood
And thought
That I could clean you up;
In the end, you were well polished
But hardly in love

Life after Kevin

We loved
And clashed;
The love came
And passed..
You blamed me
For needing room to breathe
But ever so conveniently
Overlooked your own sour deeds..
The yelling,
The control;
As if it were your own,
You stretched my soul..
Had me here,
Had me there-
Wherever you pleased;
And dangled my blessings
Before my face
As if I were designed to be teased..
You were a man
And I respected you as such;
I played your game
Even when you got rough

I took the blows,
And hide the bruises;
The people say
That the heart can't help
Who it chooses..
But,
No one has to tell me
That my well has run dry;
You have taken more
Than your share of energy
From my life..
If I don't leave now,
I will be stuck right here-
Crying over memories
As I count the years..
We loved
And clashed,
Gathered our treasures
And left them to be trashed;
Good morning to yet
Another dream
That did not last

Fight

In my mind,
I know just what to say;
In my mind,
I know that I cannot stay..
But,
These words just won't comply
And these hands just won't
Wave goodbye..
So,
Here I am once more-
Knocking at your door,
Ready to enter without a key
With intentions of restoring
You and me..
But,
The north star doesn't always
Lead the way home;
And home is not always
Where we belong..
With prosperity comes great mistakes
And not all victories are ours to take

I have seen true happiness
And watched it fold;
And have almost lost myself
While in the pursuit of that
Which is oh so nice to behold..
Not all treasures
Are meant to be confined;
And temporary pleasures
Are not worth peace of mind..
In my mind,
I know that the victory is overpriced
But sometimes,
It just feels so good
To have a reason to fight

No love from me

I can't hide,
No need to keep this a secret,
You can see right through me;
I made a promise
But, I can't keep it-
I can't love you..
Loving you is like fighting
A losing battle;
I had faith in you
But, all of that has been dismantled..
Where do I go from here?
Should I seek some sort of refuge?
My love once raged for you
Like fireworks;
But, all of those passions
Have been defused-
I would rather stumble into loneliness
Than be confused

Your back and forth,
Your temporary solutions;
I can't mold my world
Out of your ever-changing illusions..
I can't be your shining star;
All of your challenges
Have numbed by heart

Loneliness 101

Alone again,
Waiting by the phone again..
For whom,
I don't know;
But at this point,
Anything goes..
I would take the abuse,
Misuse,
Allow myself to be
Spiritually reduced..
All just to feel
A feeling that I used to know
All too well;
I want to be in love,
I want to have a story to tell..
I roam the city
With open eyes
Just to find a prize,
Someone to console,
Someone to play the role-
Of a man,
Of a king;
And once again
Give my heart a reason to sing

In the corner of this room,
I sort through my memories
Just to be aware of my past mistakes
And be prepared for the day
That he comes to me..
The wait numbs my mind
And keeps my emotions
Intertwined-
Between what used to be
As well as what the day has the power
To manifest;
The pain is severe
And it comes from my chest..
Alone again,
Ready to bend,
Needing a friend

The next page

I turned the page
Of an unfinished chapter
And sealed my loneliness
With fraudulent laughter..
Love's bruises hardly wash away
But, it is so much easier to cope
When emotions are displaced..
I dropped my anchor in a sea of tears
Just to keep a memory of recent years..
Pain and strife; bruises and bloodshed
Just to maintain a life..
It is those things that I have
Gone out of my way to accept
That keep me locked within myself..
All beauty has its moment of passing
And at some point,
All treasures must be freed;
There are those blessings
That never make it past the seed..
I turned the page
Just to get to peace of mind
But,
Nothing can ever be fully understood-
Just conquered over time

Day by day

Embarrassed by the truth,
Enticed by a lie;
False happiness fills my life..
No time taken to come to know,
No patience to grow close;
Easily overtaken
By the first promises proposed..
Far too much pain to remember
Every single tear,
A hundred faces but
I still remember every month
And year..
Every opportunity seemed so perfect,
Every circumstance seemed worth it..
Risk after risk,
Loss after loss,
Memory after memory..
Eyes,
Nose,
Lips,
Heartbeats skipped

Settling for less
Has no benefit
But,
There are things that the mouth
Just will not admit..
Chastised by reality,
Mislead by high expectations;
Inevitably,
We become the antagonist
Of our own situations

Pastime

If it is me and you,
Why is it that I am
Always left alone
As soon as you hear the phone?
If it is you and I-
If our love is supposed
To last,
Why are you always
Resorting to your past..
You are so busy repairing
What used to be
That you take away from
What you are building with me

What if you had to choose?
What if it were him or me?
Would I find myself
Lost at sea?
Is it so much to ask?
Is it so much to expect?
Why must I always pull
From the bottom of the deck?
The game that I play
Is certainly a risk
But,
I am absolutely overtaken
 By the impact of your kiss..
I am addicted to your hugs
But,
Am I truly loved?
Or am I but another pastime-
Intended to keep the one
Who truly has your heart
Off of your mind?

What you made of me

I remember the times,
I remember the moments,
I remember the miles traveled
Just to taste your love;
I gave everything
Though it was seldom enough..
Fingers to lips,
Soul to skin;
I showered you
With my treasures
Just to keep you
Satisfied within..
How young,
How innocent,
How sincere;
How desperate I was
Just to keep you here

The temper you shared,
The sorrow you dragged;
You were by no means perfect
But,
You were all I had..
And I had everything
Without having
Anything all;
Just another reason to stumble
And fall..
I fell for you
Then got back up,
Only to become content
With living in the rough..
I remember you,
I remember your lies;
I remember every night
That you made me cry..
I learned,
I lost,
I found the perfect bridge to cross..
But,
Where am I now?
Who am I now?

Appropriately to you

I heard your knock,
I heard your call;
But strangely,
I could not find the energy
To respond at all..
The only thing that
I could think of
Was all of the times
You have forsaken my love..
People sometimes change
But,
Memories cannot be rearranged..
And images of you kissing my face
Don't make up for all of the times
That you walked away..
You were everything
That I ever needed;
But,
Even needs can be disowned
After so many nights alone..
Time and time again,
I fell second to your friends;
I fell second to your lifestyle;
You chose a title over my smile

Forgive me if I seem
A little bitter
But,
There are things
That you must consider..
My giving versus your taking,
My concern versus your selfishness;
I made investments
And have reaped nothing
But stress from it..
I have offered every part me
That was mine to give;
Now,
I must give myself
A chance to live

I could be an angel

This road seems to have no end
But still,
Here I go-
Walking,
Treading softly;
Desperately attempting to catch up
To the hands of the man
That lost me..
This world keeps turning
As my heart keeps yearning..
Sooner or later,
Something has to give;
So that I can breathe,
So that I can live..
Nothing comes without sacrifice,
Nothing comes without a price
But, Lord-
I have been paying
For as long as I can remember;
And the bitterness harbored
Within my heart
Grows more and more potent
With each passing November

A little here,
A little there;
Pieces of me scattered everywhere..
Is there anyone out there
That can help me clean up
This big mess-
Help me get rid of the stress,
Encourage me to be
My best..
The money,
The jewelry,
Clothes;
It comes and goes
But,
Who out there really knows?
Who out there truly cares?
Who out there has the time to spare?
Who out there can love me
For me
And be right by my side
Even for those days when I cannot
Swallow my pride?
Free me from my shell;
I could be an angel
But,
My demons need tending as well

Freedom

Free;
A four letter word
With a simple definition-
The ability to act
At your own discretion..
But,
Who is truly free-
You?
Or me?
Do we not act in compliance
With society?
Do we not walk the walk
And dress the part,
Work to satisfy the land's expectations
Instead of that of our hearts?
Hands bribed into labor
As our legs are forced to stand;
Stressing and pushing
Just to meet management's demand

A short dollar income
Just enough to meet the payments
Of a barely suitable
Living environment;
Our gifts are goldmines
But,
We lack the confidence..
Self-doubt,
Self-pity-
Roams like a plague
Throughout the city..
Everyone needs someone
To rely on,
A rock to stand on;
But,
How often we forget
That God can give life
To anything He places
His hand on..
God has His hand on you
And I know that He has
His hand on me;
Let's come together,
Let's be free

Showtime

With his fancy clothes
And fancy shoes,
He stepped out onto the scene
With an urge to prove..
He wanted it to show,
He wanted them to know
That outer beauty was the key
To being in control..
And like a trend,
He was in..
Everyone applauded,
The encouraged his sin;
He had friends,
He had an audience,
He had evidence
That a polished body
Was more appealing
Than a polished heart;
He was the perfect example,
His level of popularity
Was off the charts

He was colorful,
He was exciting;
His image was sharp
Regardless of the lighting..
He was fun,
He was a thrill;
His impact was intense
But like most other trends,
His reign came and went..
Replaced by another darling face
Who was willing to do a little more,
Who had a little more in store
Than the one before..
And like an outdated trend,
He was placed back on the shelf
Where no one would be concerned
For what beauty he had left..
The boy thought that he could
Sell out the show
With fancy shoes
And fancy clothes
But,
That time came and went;
Now,
The curtain is closed

Take one

I wanted him to love me
But,
His mind was other places;
He had other opportunities,
Many other faces..
Silly me
To seriously think
That he would take a moment
To consider me..
He had bidders
Placing it all on the line;
While all I had to offer
Was my heart,
Soul,
And mind-
Which were surely
Insignificant treasures
To such a popular fellow..
He is happy now
And the whole world knows;
The way he pulls her close-
The love really shows

And here I am,
Left to watch-
Standing in the audience,
Reciting her lines
From the very top..
It should have been me,
It was supposed to be me
But,
He didn't spare
One single scene

Emotions & Thoughts

I must stop worrying about
What to say
And just speak my mind;
I must stop worrying
About consequences-
I am wasting time..
No dream is promised,
No treasure is worth more
Than a fulfilled soul;
And all joy is irrelevant
Without control..
I have climbed mountains
And have fallen back to Earth;
All emotions are temporary-
Even the hurt..
The days,
The moments,
The hours gone by;
Love lifts us higher-
Beyond the outline of the sky

We must press forward,
We must remain focused;
All wounds heal-
Regardless of what demons
Provoke us..
It is those roads that we prefer
That keep us going back and forth-
Between pain and prosperity;
It is easy to turn to a stranger
Because you were never there for me..
I must stop worrying about
What must be done
And just do it;
Peace is not given-
One must pursue it

Quite as blue

It's funny how the time flies;
I have memories of when
You were mine..
You were happy,
I was happy;
Together,
We were one
And there was nothing
That could have been done
To tear us apart..
I saw Heaven
When I looked into your eyes
And you saw the same
To my surprise;
I was by no means perfect
But still,
You gave your heart..
I thought that we would last,
I thought that the storms
Would past
And you would still be here

But,
You are gone
And I am here-
Starting over
Once more,
Masking my sorrow
Once more,
Wondering just what
It was all for..
You were here
To lift my up;
Now,
I am down
And no one seems to notice-
What happened?
What broke us?
Maybe one day,
I will find someone just like you
But never again
Will my skies
Be quite as blue

Tears & Romance

I took my time
And still came up short;
Misery cracked my soul
And you were the source..
Blow by blow,
Bruise by bruise,
You left me black and
And very much confused..
With the slightest shove,
I fell deeper
And with your kiss,
My heart grew weaker..
There were only urges,
No hope for me;
But, in your arms was where
I wanted to be..
I tasted your poisons
And begged for more;
I waited for hours
Outside your door-
For even a sample
Of your delight;
For your love,
I was willing to lay down my life

Emotions rushed
Through my garden
Like a battered stream;
Your embrace took
Me on journeys
Far too violent to redeem..
And here I am-
        trusting even more,
        lusting even more
        willing to love you even more
For your love,
I take it upon myself
To suffer even more

Press Play

Happiness?
Can it be found?
Or must it be built?
And how can one cope
When it begins to shift?
With time,
Comes change and circumstances
That are not always forgiven
With second chances..
Staring out of a broken window frame,
I try my best not to be consumed
By the pain..
But,
Who am I really?
What will be my legacy?
What can I possibly offer a loved one
When I am always allowing misery
To get the best of me?
When it storms,
Raindrops pierce my flesh
Like acid;
What good is faith
If it is never practiced?

I have come a long way
But,
There are still many bridges to cross;
And if I continue to stand still,
All will be lost..
How can happiness be defined
If there is no peace of mind?
And how can my blessings
Ever come to play
If I continue to press rewind?

Choosing to Love

You pretend
That you don't care at all;
You don't write
Nor do you call-
Or even look my way..
What could
I have possibly done to you
That would bring about such a change
Out of the blue-
Almost all in
One day..
Chances are
That it was me
Who brought this on;
But,
Surely you know
That it takes
More than one party
To right a wrong

Or
Maybe,
You thought that I wasn't worth
Your time;
All I wish is that
One day,
You will find-
Someone who will
Love you as much as me
And look beyond
What they see;
Because,
I saw
Bruises,
Distrust;
But still,
I chose to love

You are love

Alive-
But unaware
Of just how to live;
Lovers come
And take all
That I have to give..
Leaving me dry
On a riverside,
Vulnerable to every misery
Due to arrive..
Nothing comes
Without invitation;
And how could I
Not have welcomed you
After your conversation..
Convincing,
Promising,
And sure to stay;
The most certain circumstances
Tend to be the first to pass away

Laughing-
With no reason to smile at all;
Through your embrace,
I surrender without withdrawal..
You are love
And your game will never change;
You broadcast happiness
Then present your pain

Revelation

You swore
That you would be different
From those that I have loved before;
And you were right-
You hurt me even more..
I had hope
But,
It is so difficult to cope
When you whisper promises
Under your breath
But your actions
Scream something else..
I danced according to your rhythm,
I molded my emotions
So that you could feel them..
But still,
You were unsatisfied;
Quietly,
You walked out of my life..
I dream of the way
That you used to hold me;
If you were unhappy,
You should have told me

Lord knows
That I tried and tried
But still,
My effort was denied..
You swore
That you would be different
And it is your embrace
That has hindered my deliverance..
You planted seeds of delight
And before my eyes,
You left them to dry..
The fruit is gone
As well as my song

The gift of life

Answers unknown;
Nothing is solid
When you're all alone;
Arms were open
But,
The chemistry was wrong..
I swallowed my pride
A long time ago;
But in the darkness,
Love doesn't flow..
I kept my gold,
Printed the balance
And paid with my soul;
Before it is all done,
My tears will be all
That is left to behold..
Hundreds of bridges to cross,
I set my own traps
And like that,
I am caught-
Designated to be lost
By the pleasures
That I have sought

A prisoner of me
To an infinite degree
With intentions
To love
As well as to please..
Lessons unlearned;
Happiness comes to be
Then,
It is gone;
Life is a gift
But,
It is not ours to own

Their influence

I met anxious
And she introduced me to lonely;
Together,
They learned just how
To control me..
They were the best of friends;
And like a popular crowd,
They lured me in..
Like a sour breeze
On a summer day,
They changed my motion-
Redirected my steps,
Taught me to be loyal
Even when I was offered no devotion..
I dared to seek
And complained
When I could not find;
There seemed to be
Many questions
With little time

What I thought to be love,
Turned out to be
Yet another fire
Burning on the riverside-
Glowing oh so bright
Until the waking of the tide..
And like a child,
I was raised to believe
Familiar stories
Instead of trusting
The treasures
That were right before me..
I cherished anxious
And gave everything to lonely;
I was so busy looking to myself
That I forgot to make room
For anyone to console me

A little too late

He fights to convince me
That he is the one
As I look forward
To the lies
That I know will come..
Promises pour like blessings
Upon the land;
But,
How seldom does he not
Greet me at the door
With an empty hand..
He makes room
For me to take my place
And I shed tears
As he caresses my face..
So many memories,
So many reasons to submit;
But sometimes,
Even sincere actions
Can be deemed inadequate..
I turn to him
With concern
And he swears
That I will learn

But,
I cannot bear another useless lesson
That dares to challenge
My personal perception-
Of life,
Of joy,
Of the treasures
That my demons have fought
Ever so diligently
To destroy..
He stands his ground
Just to win my heart;
But,
No man can truly have victory
Over that which
The world has already
Torn apart

Nothing matters

In this huge world,
It is rather puzzling how
I can still walk across the grass
And feel a loneliness
That no other man can grasp..
From the side windows of my home,
I see stars and trees
And hands that used to hold my own..
Though sorrow grows
From the words that I never said,
Seldom do I find a reason
To crawl out of bed..
Here,
I am safe from becoming a waste
Of yet another traveling face
That not even my devotion
Can convince to be still;
All hearts eventually act
In the best interest
Of their own will

All I want is happiness,
A destiny,
Someone to keep all of the promises
Confessed to me..
In this huge world,
I cannot help but feel small;
Without love,
Nothing matters at all

Dear Love

Dear love,
Can't you hear
The people calling for you?
Dear love,
Can't you see
What we're going through?
The constant disappointments,
Change after change;
Fragile hearts doomed
To never be the same..
The bruises we take
For the love we make;
It presses downward on fibers of hope
That are itching to break..
One night of tears
Welcomes sorrow
That will linger for years..
And lead us to cross lines
That we never drew;
All while embarking on a
Seemingly hopeless journey
Of our opinions of true

Up and down,
Back and forth;
We circle around happiness
But rarely find the source..
We are lost,
We are demanding;
We state our claims
Without proper understanding..
We are everything but free-
Mere rolling stones
That are headed for the sea..
Dear love,
The people are opening their hearts;
We are ready for action
But,
Where do we start?

Heaven-sent

 It was a kiss that could have
Given life,
A touch that I had never felt;
A yearning that made me mold myself
Into the very being that you called for;
In a matter of moments,
You became the one who
I would have given my all for..
A conversation
That challenged my mind,
A thirst that had me going back
And forth through time..
All to find a treasure-
So angelic that it could have
Brought worlds together..
It was you,
You and your eyes of dazzling blue
Who took the time to climb down
From the mountain peak
And save me from the valley
Where blessings were hard to keep

It is you
Who escorted me into today
And keeps me steady
Whenever my heart
Begins to stray..
And now we are here
In paradise;
Taking on the world,
Building a life-
Along with memories
That keep us going

for everything
in life,
there comes a price
but,
is the lifestyle worth
the debt?

DEDICATION:

This book is dedicated
To my good friend
Dana Melton-Chilcutt
Who always keeps me going with her
Laughter, warm spirit, life stories, and
Wisdom. You are truly a blessing to
Me..

Love always,
Kentrell

all at once

www.ingramcontent.com/pod-product-compliance
Lightning Source LLC
Chambersburg PA
CBHW020521030426
42337CB00011B/491